# Edgard Varèse

# DENSITY 21.5

## for flute alone

# RICORDI

# DENSITY 21.5*

**Flute Solo**

EDGARD VARÈSE

* Written in January, 1936, at the request of Georges Barrère for the inauguration of his platinum flute. Revised April, 1946. 21.5 is the density of platinum.

** Always strictly in time—follow metronomic indications.

*** Notes marked + to be played softly, hitting the keys at the same time to produce a percussive effect.